Give a Hug...
Get a Hug™
with GivaGeta Smiles™

A Children's Book About Giving and Getting Hugs, Giggles, Kindness, and More

Written by:
James Louis Cantoni, Sr.
Jackie Cantoni

Illustrated by:
Maribeth Blonski

A portion of your purchase goes to the GivaGeta Foundation to help children with special needs in tribute to Nathan Cantoni.

Hop on in
for hugs, giggles,
friendship, and more.

Published by Realizing Dreams, Inc
Punta Gorda, Florida
All rights reserved.

For information, reproduction, or bulk purchases, please email:

mydreams@RealizingDreams.us

ISBN: 978-0-9903128-7-1
Library of Congress Control Number: 2019910282

Hugs to James and Nathan ~

Love,
Mom and Dad

Meet the forest friends...

Give a Hug... Get a Hug™

Beautiful Butterfly™

Endearing friends spread kindness and friendship as they give and get hugs smiles, winks, butterfly kisses, giggles, a hand to hold, and more.

Giggly Gecko™

Respectful Racoon™

Responsible Rabbit™

Teamwork Turtle™

Buddy Bear™

Flexible Fox™

Confident Chipmunk™

Marvelous Mouse™

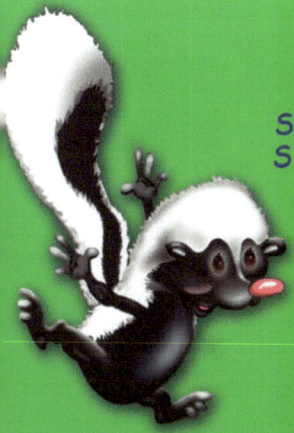

Bright Blue Bird™

Sincere Skunk™

Optimistic Owl™

Magnificent Moose™

Friendship Frog™

Dependable Deer™

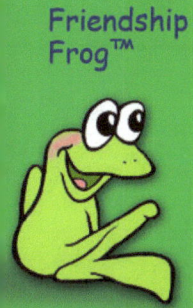

Give a hug ...

Get a hug™

...GivaGeta™

Give a butterfly kiss...

Get a butterfly kiss™

...GivaGeta™

Give a tickle...

Get a tickle™

...GivaGeta™

Give a giggle...

Hee Hee Hee

Get a giggle™

...GivaGeta™

Give a hand to hold...

Get a hand to hold™

...GivaGeta™

Give a wink...

Get a wink™

...GivaGeta™

Give an Eskimo kiss...

Get an Eskimo kiss™

...GivaGeta™

Give friendship...

Get friendship™

...GivaGeta™

Give a whistle...

Get a whistle™

...GivaGeta™

Give a laugh...

Get a kiss™

...GivaGeta™

Give kindness...

Get kindness™

…GivaGeta™

Give a song...

Laa La Laa Laaaa

Get a along™

...GivaGeta™

Give an I love you...

Get an I love you™

...GivaGeta™

Give a Hug... Get a Hug™

It was FUN to give and get hugs, giggles, friendship, and I love you's with you.

I know you will be a kind friend who grows up knowing that when you give you get more in return... and the more in return is that good feeling inside from giving!

Beautiful Butterfly™

Giggly Gecko™

Buddy Bear™

Respectful Racoon™

Responsible Rabbit™

Flexible Fox™

Confident Chipmunk™

Teamwork Turtle™

Marvelous Mouse™

Bright Blue Bird™

Sincere Skunk™

Optimistic Owl™

Magnificent Moose™

Friendship Frog™

Dependable Deer™

THE END

THANKS FOR
HOPPING ON IN!

What's GivaGeta?

Give a Smile ... Get a Smile ... GivaGeta.™ It's a true story of a little girl named Jackie who would dot the "i" in her name with a special smile on the notes she wrote. In doing so, she learned kindness at a young age. Today, Jackie is all grown up and believes people have the power to create a kinder world by doing the little things such as sharing "GivaGeta's" that inspire us to think of others in a fun filled way.

Give a smile ... Get a smile™, Give kindness ... Get kindness,™ Give friendship ... Get friendship,™ caring, understanding and more are the fun "GivaGeta" ways to give and get smiles and share kind messages and values.

Jackie and her husband Jim named her smiley **"GivaGeta Smiles."** Together they created The GivaGeta Collection of products which spread positive inspiration in a way that people remember throughout their lives.

Our Mission:

To spread more smiles, kindness and understanding throughout the world, one person at a time.

Help Kids ™

Thank You!

Your purchase is helping spread more smiles,
kindness, understanding, and "I love you's" throughout the world.

A portion of every GivaGeta Smiles purchase goes to
The GivaGeta Foundation to help children with special needs
in tribute to the founder's son Nathan.

The GivaGeta Foundation:

The GivaGeta Foundation was created because of life experiences
with Nathan who requires extra love and care as he cannot walk, talk
or see. Nathan's smiles and giggles are contagious and that's his way
to bring smiles and laughter to others. God gave Jackie and Jim a
beautiful little boy whose way of communication shows the gift of a smile.

www.GivaGeta.org

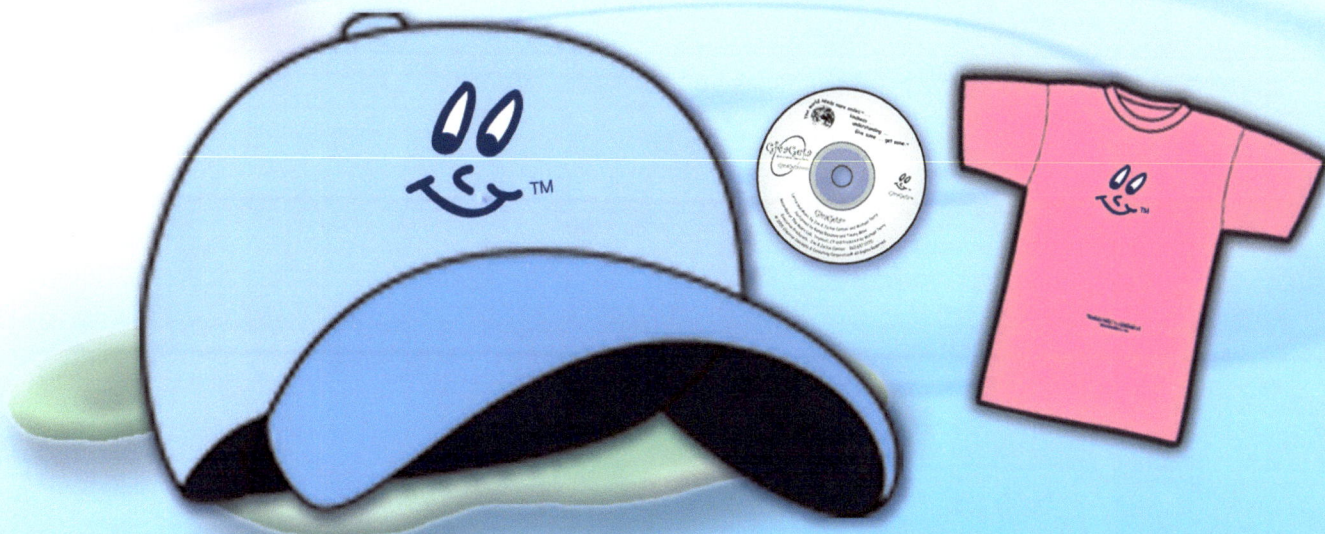

www.ingramcontent.com/pod-product-compliance
Lightning Source LLC
Chambersburg PA
CBHW041549040426
42447CB00002B/115

www.ingramcontent.com/pod-product-compliance
Lightning Source LLC
Chambersburg PA
CBHW041548040426
42447CB00002B/95